foreword

Place a juicy piece of sirloin or rib eye on a hot grill and the sound says: Supper's soon and it's going to be terrific.

At Company's Coming, we know great steaks, and we've collected some of our best recipes so you can make them too. Complete with fabulous marinades, sauces, rubs and salsas, this handy book is just the thing to take to the cottage or cabin, or tuck beside the barbecue.

And if it's too cold to step out onto the deck, don't worry. The cooking times for a gas barbecue on **high** or **medium-high** are the same for the broiler on the top rack (with two exceptions, indicated in the recipes' introductions). If it says to barbecue on **medium**, just reduce your broil time by a minute. We've also included recipes for the frying pan and the electric grill—different ways to enjoy the distinctive sizzle and savour of a delicious steak.

Jean Paré

beef benedict

The classic Eggs Benedict recipe calls for Hollandaise sauce, but our beefed-up version pairs well with this more robust Béarnaise, flavoured with vinegar, tarragon and cayenne. While making the steak be careful not to overheat the sauce or it will curdle.

BÉARNAISE SAUCE

Dry (or alcohol-free) white wine	1 cup	250 mL
Finely chopped shallots (or green onion)	2 tbsp.	30 mL
White wine vinegar	2 tbsp.	30 mL
Dried tarragon, crushed	2 tsp.	10 mL
Pepper (white is best)	1/4 tsp.	1 mL
Egg yolks, large	4	4
Hard margarine (or butter), melted	2 tbsp.	30 mL
Hard margarine (or butter), melted	6 tbsp.	100 mL
Finely chopped fresh parsley (or 1/2 tsp., 2 mL, flakes)	2 tsp.	10 mL
Cayenne pepper, sprinkle		

BEEF BENEDICT

Beef rib-eye (or sirloin) steak	1 1/2 lbs.	680 g
English muffins, split and toasted	3	3
Large eggs, poached	6	6
Paprika, sprinkle		
Sprigs of fresh parsley, for garnish		
Orange slices, for garnish		

Béarnaise Sauce: Combine first 5 ingredients in small saucepan. Bring to a boil. Reduce heat to medium-low. Simmer, uncovered, for 8 to 10 minutes until liquid is reduced to about 2/3 cup (150 mL). Strain into small cup. Discard shallots.

Whisk egg yolks in top of double boiler or heatproof bowl set on saucepan over simmering water on medium-high. Whisk in first amount of melted margarine. Whisk in wine mixture and second amount of margarine. Stir constantly with whisk until fluffy and thickened. Remove from heat.

Add parsley and cayenne pepper. Stir. Makes about 1 1/2 cups (375 mL) sauce. Cover to keep warm.

Beef Benedict: Preheat electric grill for 5 minutes. Cook steak on greased grill for about 5 minutes per side until desired doneness. Transfer to cutting board. Cover with foil. Let stand for 10 minutes. Cut steak across the grain into 1/4 inch (6 mm) slices.

Arrange on English muffin halves. Carefully place 1 egg over each. Spoon Béarnaise Sauce over top. Sprinkle with paprika.

Garnish with parsley sprigs and orange slices. Serves 6.

1 serving: 554 Calories; 36.7 g Total Fat (9.2 g Mono, 1.9 g Poly, 10.6 g Sat); 425 mg Cholesterol; 15 g Carbohydrate; 1 g Fibre; 32 g Protein; 383 mg Sodium

grilled steak sandwiches

Buy twice the steaks and make a double batch of marinade. Freeze extra steaks in marinade for a busy day—just pop the frozen meat in your fridge to thaw that morning.

FAVOURITE STEAK MARINADE

Brown sugar, packed	3 tbsp.	50 mL
Lemon juice	2 tbsp.	30 mL
Soy sauce	2 tbsp.	30 mL
Water	2 tbsp.	30 mL
Ketchup	1 tbsp.	15 mL
Garlic clove, minced (or 1/4 tsp., 1 mL, powder)	1	1
Ground ginger	1/4 tsp.	1 mL

SANDWICH

Beef rib-eye steaks, trimmed of fat	1 lb.	454 g
Cooking oil	1 tbsp.	15 mL
Sliced onion	2 cups	500 mL
Sliced fresh white mushrooms	2 cups	500 mL
Kaiser rolls, split	4	4
Hard margarine (or butter), softened	2 tbsp.	30 mL
Light sour cream	1/2 cup	125 mL
Dijon mustard (with whole seeds)	2 tbsp.	30 mL
Fresh spinach leaves, lightly packed	2 cups	500 mL
Medium yellow pepper, thinly sliced	1	1
Swiss cheese slices	4	4

Favourite Steak Marinade: Measure all 7 ingredients into small bowl. Stir until brown sugar is dissolved. Makes about 1/2 cup (125 mL) marinade.

Sandwich: Put steaks into large resealable freezer bag. Add marinade. Seal bag. Turn until coated. Let stand in refrigerator for at least 6 hours or overnight, turning occasionally. Remove steak. Preheat gas barbecue to medium. Cook steaks on greased grill for about 5 minutes per side until desired doneness. Transfer to cutting board. Cover with foil. Let stand for 10 minutes. Cut steaks across the grain into 1/4 inch (6 mm) slices.

Heat cooking oil in large frying pan on medium. Add onion. Cook for about 10 minutes, stirring occasionally, until softened. Increase heat to medium-high.

Add mushrooms. Cook for about 5 minutes, stirring occasionally, until liquid is evaporated.

Spread cut sides of rolls with margarine. Heat on grill, cut-side down, over medium heat for about 3 minutes until golden. Cover to keep warm.

Combine sour cream and mustard in separate small bowl. Spread on bottom halves of rolls. Layer remaining 3 ingredients, steak and mushroom mixture over sour cream mixture. Cover with top halves of rolls. Makes 4 sandwiches.

1 sandwich: 606 Calories; 28.6 g Total Fat (12.5 g Mono, 3.6 g Poly, 12 g Sat); 79 mg Cholesterol; 49 g Carbohydrate; 3 g Fibre; 39 g Protein; 1283 mg Sodium

mushroom steak sandwiches

A fabulous mix of garlicky mushrooms (great as an easy side dish for other barbecued entrees), spinach salad and grilled beef on a bun—delicious!

Sliced fresh white mushrooms	2 cups	500 mL
Garlic clove, minced (or 1/4 tsp., 1 mL, powder)	1	1
Montreal steak spice	1/4 tsp.	1 mL
Montreal steak spice	1/2 tsp.	2 mL
Beef strip loin steak	1 lb.	454 g
Light mayonnaise	2 tbsp.	30 mL
Sesame (or cooking) oil	1 tbsp.	15 mL
Finely grated gingerroot (or 1/8 tsp., 0.5 mL, ground ginger)	1/2 tsp.	2 mL
Chopped fresh spinach leaves, lightly packed	2 cups	500 mL
Whole wheat kaiser rolls, split	4	4

Preheat gas barbecue to medium-high. Place mushrooms and garlic on 18 inch (45 cm) long sheet of heavy-duty (or double layer of regular) foil. Sprinkle with first amount of steak spice. Fold edges of foil together over mushrooms to enclose. Fold ends to seal completely. Place on grill, seam-side up.

Sprinkle second amount of steak spice on steak. Cook on greased grill for 4 to 5 minutes per side until desired doneness. Transfer to cutting board. Cover with foil. Let stand for 10 minutes. Cut steak across the grain into 1/8 inch (3 mm) slices. Remove mushroom packet from grill.

Combine next 3 ingredients in small bowl. Add spinach. Toss until coated.

Arrange spinach mixture on bottom halves of rolls. Arrange steak slices over spinach. Spoon mushrooms over steak. Cover with top halves of rolls. Makes 4 sandwiches.

1 sandwich: 494 Calories; 29.0 g Total Fat (10.8 g Mono, 3.4 g Poly, 9.6 g Sat); 79 mg Cholesterol; 32 g Carbohydrate; 5 g Fibre; 28 g Protein; 534 mg Sodium

steak fajitas

Add a dab of deli guacamole to these wraps (pronounced fa-HEE-tas) for even more Tex-Mex flavour!

TEX-MEX MARINADE

Beer	1/2 cup	125 mL
Lime juice	1/4 cup	60 mL
Water	1/4 cup	60 mL
Garlic cloves, minced (or 1/2 tsp. 2 mL, powder)	2	2
Cajun seasoning	1 tsp.	5 mL
Pepper, sprinkle		

FAJITAS

Flank steak (scored on 1 side)	1 1/4 lbs.	560 g
Cooking oil	1 tbsp.	15 mL
Large onions, cut into 1/2 inch (12 mm) slices	2	2
Medium red pepper, quartered	1	1
Medium yellow pepper, quartered	1	1
Flour tortillas (8 inch, 20 cm, diameter), warmed	8	8

Tex-Mex Marinade: Combine all 6 ingredients in small bowl. Makes about 1 cup (250 mL) marinade.

Fajitas: Put steak into large resealable plastic bag. Add half of marinade. Reserve remaining marinade. Seal bag. Turn until coated. Let stand in refrigerator for at least 6 hours or overnight, turning occasionally.

Remove steak. Discard used marinade. Preheat electric grill for 5 minutes. Cook on greased grill for 10 minutes per side. Transfer to cutting board. Brush with 1 tbsp. (15 mL) reserved marinade. Cover with foil. Let stand for 10 minutes.

Combine remaining marinade with cooking oil.

Cook next 3 ingredients on hot grill, turning occasionally and brushing with oil mixture, until tender-crisp. Transfer vegetables to cutting board. Slice red and yellow peppers. Cut onion slices into quarters. Cut steak across the grain into 1/4 inch (6 mm) thick slices.

Arrange steak and vegetables down centre of tortillas. Fold bottom ends of tortillas over filling. Fold in sides, slightly overlapping, leaving top ends open. Makes 8 fajitas.

1 fajita: 325 Calories; 11.8 g Total Fat (5.5 g Mono, 1.6 g Poly, 3.7 g Sat); 30 mg Cholesterol; 33 g Carbohydrate; 2 g Fibre; 20 g Protein; 424 mg Sodium

mango beef salad

The Maple Dressing can be made up to five days before; just keep it in the fridge in an air-tight container.

Lemon pepper	1 tbsp.	15 mL
Olive (or cooking) oil	2 tsp.	10 mL
Garlic clove, minced (or 1/4 tsp., 1 mL, powder)	1	1
Beef strip loin steaks	1 1/4 lb.	560 g
Mixed salad greens, lightly packed	5 cups	1.25 L
Can of sliced mango in syrup, drained and coarsely chopped	14 oz.	398 mL
Cashews, toasted (see Tip, page 64) and coarsely chopped	1/2 cup	125 mL
Bacon slices, cooked crisp and crumbled	8	8
MAPLE DRESSING		
Peanut (or cooking) oil	1/3 cup	75 mL
Maple (or maple-flavoured) syrup	2 tbsp.	30 mL
Red wine vinegar	2 tbsp.	30 mL
Soy sauce	2 tsp.	10 mL
Salt	1/4 tsp.	1 mL

Combine first 3 ingredients in small bowl.

Spread oil mixture on both sides of steaks. Preheat barbecue to medium-high. Cook steaks on greased grill for about 5 minutes per side until desired doneness. Transfer to cutting board. Cover with foil. Let stand for 10 minutes. Cut across the grain into 1/8 inch (3 mm) thick slices. Transfer to large bowl.

Add next 4 ingredients. Toss gently.

Maple Dressing: Combine all 5 ingredients in jar with tight-fitting lid. Shake well. Makes about 2/3 cup (150 mL) dressing. Pour over steak mixture. Toss gently. Makes about 11 cups (2.75 L). Serves 8.

1 serving: 313 Calories; 22.7 g Total Fat (11.2 g Mono, 4.4 g Poly, 5.6 g Sat); 37 mg Cholesterol; 12 g Carbohydrate; 1 g Fibre; 16 g Protein; 740 mg Sodium

beef fajita salad

This recipe makes four steaks go a long way. If you're counting calories, use low-fat dressing and sour cream.

Taco seasoning mix, stir before measuring	2 tbsp.	30 mL
Beef strip loin steaks	1 lb.	454 g
Mixed salad greens, lightly packed	12 cups	3 L
Ripe medium avocados, sliced	2	2
Medium red onion, sliced	1	1
Ranch dressing	1 cup	250 mL
Sour cream	1/2 cup	125 mL
Salsa	2/3 cup	150 mL
Corn chips, coarsely crushed	2 cups	500 mL
Can of sliced jalapeño peppers, drained	4 oz.	114 mL

Preheat gas barbecue to medium-high. Rub seasoning mix on both sides of steaks. Cook on greased grill for 3 to 5 minutes per side until desired doneness. Transfer to cutting board. Cover with foil. Let stand for 10 minutes. Cut across the grain into 1/8 inch (3 mm) thick slices.

Put next 3 ingredients into large bowl. Toss. Arrange on 8 serving plates. Arrange steak over top.

Drizzle with dressing and sour cream. Spoon salsa over top.

Sprinkle with corn chips and jalapeño peppers. Serves 8.

1 serving: 849 Calories; 63.3 g Total Fat (13.1 g Mono, 14.1 g Poly, 13.6 g Sat); 77 mg Cholesterol; 42 g Carbohydrate; 6 g Fibre; 31 g Protein; 1032 mg Sodium

beef and mandarin salad

The dressing for this colourful, fresh salad can be made two days ahead.

Beef inside round steak, trimmed of fat	3/4 lb.	340 g
Garlic salt	1/2 tsp.	2 mL
Mixed salad greens, lightly packed	6 cups	1.5 L
Can of mandarin orange segments, drained	10 oz.	284 mL
Thinly sliced red onion	1/2 cup	125 mL
Thinly sliced red pepper	1/2 cup	125 mL
SWEET PARMESAN DRESSING		
Finely grated Parmesan cheese	2 tbsp.	30 mL
Lemon juice	2 tbsp.	30 mL
Olive (or cooking) oil	2 tbsp.	30 mL
Liquid honey	2 tsp.	10 mL
Garlic clove, minced (or 1/4 tsp., 1 mL, powder)	1	1
Pepper	1/4 tsp.	1 mL
Salt (optional)	1/4 tsp.	1 mL

Sprinkle both sides of steak with garlic salt. Preheat electric grill for 5 minutes or gas barbecue to medium-high. Cook steak on greased grill for about 5 minutes per side until desired doneness. Transfer to cutting board. Cover with foil. Let stand for 10 minutes. Cut across the grain into 1/4 inch (6 mm) thick slices.

Put next 4 ingredients into large bowl. Add beef. Toss.

Sweet Parmesan Dressing: Combine all 7 ingredients in jar with tight-fitting lid. Shake well. Makes about 1/3 cup (75 mL) dressing. Drizzle over salad. Toss gently. Makes about 6 cups (1.5 L). Serves 4.

1 serving: 222 Calories; 10.2 g Total Fat (6.2 g Mono, 0.8 g Poly, 2.3 g Sat); 39 mg Cholesterol; 14 g Carbohydrate; 2 g Fibre; 20 g Protein; 247 mg Sodium

crisp minted salad

A vibrant combination of crisp vegetables complements tender strips of beef coated with spicy mint dressing.

Beef rib-eye (or top sirloin) steak, trimmed of fat	1/2 lb.	225 g
Salt	1/4 tsp.	1 mL
Pepper	1/8 tsp.	0.5 mL
Fresh bean sprouts	1 cup	250 mL
Sliced English cucumber (with peel)	1 cup	250 mL
Thinly sliced red pepper	1 cup	250 mL
Thinly sliced red onion	1/4 cup	60 mL
MINTY LIME DRESSING		
Canola oil	2 tbsp.	30 mL
Chopped fresh mint (or 1 1/2 tsp., 7 mL, dried)	2 tbsp.	30 mL
Lime juice	2 tbsp.	30 mL
Chili paste (sambal oelek)	1/2 tsp.	2 mL
Granulated sugar	1/2 tsp.	2 mL
Sesame oil, for flavour	1/2 tsp.	2 mL
Salt	1/4 tsp.	1 mL

Place steak in shallow baking dish. Sprinkle with salt and pepper. Chill, covered, for 1 hour. Preheat electric grill for 5 minutes or gas barbecue to medium. Cook steak on greased grill for about 4 minutes per side until desired doneness. Transfer to cutting board. Cover with foil. Let stand for 10 minutes. Cut across the grain into 1/8 inch (3 mm) thick slices. Transfer to large bowl.

Add next 4 ingredients. Toss.

Minty Lime Dressing: Combine all 7 ingredients in jar with tight-fitting lid. Shake well. Makes about 1/3 cup (75 mL) dressing. Drizzle over beef mixture. Toss. Makes about 4 cups (1 L). Serves 2.

1 serving: 368 Calories; 22.9 g Total Fat (11.9 g Mono, 5 g Poly, 4.2 g Sat); 54 mg Cholesterol; 14 g Carbohydrate; 3 g Fibre; 28 g Protein; 670 mg Sodium

barbecue party salad

Let your guests slice and dice while you do the barbecuing!

Dijon mustard	2 tbsp.	30 mL
Pepper	1 tsp.	5 mL
Beef top sirloin steak	2 lbs.	900 g
Medium red peppers	3	3
Medium corncobs, husked	2	2
Olive (or cooking) oil	1 1/2 tbsp.	25 mL
Medium zucchini (with peel), halved	2	2
Red onions, cut into 1/4 inch (6 mm) slices	2	2
Olive (or cooking) oil	1 1/2 tbsp.	25 mL
Medium tomatoes, diced	2	2
Sliced black olives	1/2 cup	125 mL
BALSAMIC DRESSING		
Olive (or cooking) oil	1/3 cup	75 mL
Balsamic vinegar	3 tbsp.	50 mL
Chopped fresh chives	3 tbsp.	50 mL
Chopped fresh parsley	3 tbsp.	50 mL
Garlic cloves, minced	2	2
Salt	1 1/2 tsp.	7 mL
Pepper	1/2 tsp.	2 mL
Mixed salad greens, lightly packed	4 cups	1 L

Combine mustard and pepper in small bowl. Spread on both sides of steak. Preheat gas barbecue to medium-high. Cook steak on greased grill for 8 to 10 minutes per side until desired doneness. Transfer to cutting board. Cover with foil. Let stand for 10 minutes. Set aside.

Place red peppers on greased grill. Cook for about 10 minutes, turning occasionally, until skins are blistered and blackened. Transfer to medium bowl. Cover with plastic wrap. Let sweat for 15 minutes until cool enough to handle. Remove and discard skins. Chop. Set aside.

Brush corncobs with first amount of olive oil. Reduce heat to medium. Cook cobs on grill for about 10 minutes, turning occasionally, until grill marks appear and kernels start to crackle. Transfer to cutting board. Cool slightly. Cut kernels off cobs with sharp knife. Place in extra-large bowl. Add red pepper.

Brush zucchini and onion with second amount of olive oil. Cook on grill for 12 to 15 minutes, turning occasionally, until grill marks appear and vegetables are tender-crisp. Transfer to cutting board. Chop. Add to corn mixture. Stir.

Add tomato and olives. Stir.

Balsamic Dressing: Combine all 7 ingredients in jar with tight-fitting lid. Shake well. Makes about 2/3 cup (150 mL) dressing. Drizzle over vegetable mixture. Toss. Cut steak across the grain into 1/4 inch (6 mm) thick slices. Slice crosswise into 1 inch (2.5 cm) strips. Add to vegetable mixture. Toss.

Add salad greens. Toss. Serves 8.

1 serving: 323 Calories; 19.6 g Total Fat (12.7 Mono, 1.8 Poly, 3.7 Sat); 53 mg Cholesterol; 14 g Carbohydrate; 3 g Fibre; 25 g Protein; 444 mg Sodium

mexican flatbread pizza

As a variation, omit the flatbread and serve the steak and toppings in taco shells or wrapped in tortillas.

Flatbread (or prebaked pizza crust), 12 inch (30 cm) diameter	1	1
Chunky salsa	1/2 cup	125 mL
Lime juice	2 tbsp.	30 mL
Beef minute (or fast-fry) steak	1 lb.	454 g
Chunky salsa	1/2 cup	125 mL
Grated medium Cheddar cheese	1/4 cup	60 mL
Grated Monterey Jack cheese	1/4 cup	60 mL

Place flatbread on ungreased baking sheet. Bake in 250°F (120°C) oven for about 30 minutes until warm.

Combine first amount of salsa and lime juice in medium bowl. Add steak. Turn to coat. Let stand for 15 minutes. Drain and discard salsa mixture. Heat large frying pan on medium-high. Add steak. Cook for about 2 minutes per side until desired doneness. Transfer to cutting board. Cover with foil. Let stand for 10 minutes. Cut across the grain into 1/8 inch (3 mm) thick slices.

Spread second amount of salsa on flatbread almost to edge. Arrange steak over top. Sprinkle with Cheddar and Monterey Jack cheeses. Broil on top rack in oven for about 2 minutes until cheese is melted. Cuts into 8 wedges.

1 wedge: 136 Calories; 5.6 g Total Fat (1.8 g Mono, 0.2 g Poly, 2.6 g Sat); 41 mg Cholesterol; 6 g Carbohydrate; 1 g Fibre; 15 g Protein; 325 mg Sodium

sirloin sizzle

A salad and baked potatoes are all you need with this juicy steak for a great dinner.

Beef top sirloin steak, trimmed of fat	1 lb.	454 g
CIDER MOLASSES MARINADE		
Apple cider vinegar	3 tbsp.	50 mL
Ketchup	2 tbsp.	30 mL
Fancy (mild) molasses	1 tbsp.	15 mL
Steak sauce	1 tbsp.	15 mL
Dried oregano	1 tsp.	5 mL
Garlic clove, minced (or 1/4 tsp., 1 mL, powder)	1	1
Pepper	1/4 tsp.	1 mL
Ground cinnamon	1/8 tsp.	0.5 mL

Put steak into shallow baking dish.

Cider Molasses Marinade: Combine all 8 ingredients in small bowl. Makes about 1/2 cup (125 mL) marinade. Transfer 1 tbsp. (15 mL) to small dish. Pour remaining marinade over steak. Turn to coat. Let stand for 10 minutes. Remove steak. Transfer marinade to small saucepan. Bring to a boil. Reduce heat to medium-low. Simmer, uncovered, for 5 minutes. Preheat gas barbecue to medium. Cook steak on greased grill for about 5 minutes per side until desired doneness. Transfer to cutting board. Brush with reserved marinade. Cover with foil. Let stand for 10 minutes. Cut into 4 equal portions. Serves 4.

1 serving: 204 Calories; 8.1 g Total Fat (3.3 g Mono, 0.3 g Poly, 3.1 g Sat); 60 mg Cholesterol; 7 g Carbohydrate; trace Fibre; 25 g Protein; 196 mg Sodium

margarita marinated steak

Give a less tender cut of meat the spa treatment with a long soak in this refreshing lime marinade. A pitcher of margaritas (lime, of course!) would make a fun starter.

MARGARITA MARINADE

Frozen concentrated limeade, thawed	1/3 cup	75 mL
Water	1/3 cup	75 mL
Chopped fresh cilantro	1/4 cup	60 mL
Cooking oil	1/4 cup	60 mL
Cajun seasoning	3 tbsp.	50 mL
Garlic cloves, minced (or 3/4 tsp., 4 mL, powder)	3	3
Ground cumin	1 tsp.	5 mL

STEAK

Boneless beef round steak, trimmed of fat	1 1/2 lbs.	680 g
Chopped avocado	1 cup	250 mL
Chopped orange	3/4 cup	175 mL
Finely chopped red onion	1/4 cup	60 mL

Margarita Marinade: Combine all 7 ingredients in small bowl. Reserve 2 tbsp. (30 mL) in small cup. Makes about 1 1/4 cups (300 mL) marinade.

Steak: Put steak into large resealable freezer bag. Add remaining marinade. Seal bag. Turn until coated. Let stand in refrigerator for at least 6 hours or overnight, turning occasionally. Preheat gas barbecue to medium. Cook steak on greased grill for about 3 minutes per side or until desired doneness. Transfer to cutting board. Cover with foil. Let stand for 10 minutes.

Combine remaining 3 ingredients in small bowl. Add reserved marinade. Toss until coated. Cut steak across the grain into 1/4 inch (6 mm) slices. Arrange on large serving plate. Top with avocado mixture. Serves 6.

1 serving: 268 Calories; 13.7 g Total Fat (7.1 g Mono, 1.4 g Poly, 3.8 g Sat); 55 mg Cholesterol; 8 g Carbohydrate; 2 g Fibre; 28 g Protein; 269 mg Sodium

sweet and sour steak

Here's a fast, tasty entree that's on the table in minutes.

CHUT-ECUE SAUCE

Sweet and sour barbecue sauce	1/2 cup	125 mL
Finely chopped onion	1/4 cup	60 mL
Mild (or hot) chutney	1/4 cup	60 mL
Soy sauce	1 tbsp.	15 mL
Cooking oil	1 tsp.	5 mL
Beef eye of round (or sirloin tip) steak, cut into 4 pieces	1 lb.	454 g

Chut-ecue Sauce: Combine all 4 ingredients in small bowl. Makes about 1 cup (250 mL) sauce.

Heat cooking oil in large frying pan on medium-high. Add steak. Cook for 1 to 2 minutes until browned. Reduce heat to medium-low. Spoon sauce over steak. Simmer, uncovered, for 6 to 10 minutes, turning once, until desired doneness. Serves 4.

1 serving: 849 Calories; 63.3 g Total Fat (13.1 g Mono, 14.1 g Poly, 13.6 g Sat); 77 mg Cholesterol; 42 g Carbohydrate; 6 g Fibre; 31 g Protein; 1032 mg Sodium

lemon garlic steaks

Pop the strip loin into the marinade in the morning to give it time to absorb the lemon and garlic flavours. Serve with potato wedges and a fresh garden salad.

LEMON GARLIC MARINADE		
Chopped fresh parsley	1/4 cup	60 mL
Lemon juice	3 tbsp.	50 mL
Sweet (or regular) chili sauce	2 tbsp.	30 mL
Olive (or cooking) oil	1 tbsp.	15 mL
Garlic cloves, minced (or 1/2 tsp., 2 mL, powder)	2	2
Pepper	1 tsp.	5 mL
Beef strip loin steak, trimmed of fat and cut into 4 pieces	1 lb.	454 g

Lemon Garlic Marinade: Combine all 6 ingredients in small bowl. Makes about 1/2 cup (125 mL) marinade.

Put steak into large resealable freezer bag. Add marinade. Seal bag. Turn until coated. Let stand in refrigerator for at least 6 hours or overnight, turning occasionally. Remove steak. Preheat electric grill for 5 minutes or gas barbecue to medium-high. Cook steak on greased grill for about 5 minutes per side until desired doneness. Transfer to plate. Cover with foil. Let stand for 10 minutes. Serves 4.

1 serving: 203 Calories; 12.1 g Total Fat (5.6 g Mono, 0.5 g Poly, 4.4 g Sat); 46 mg Cholesterol; 2 g Carbohydrate; trace Fibre; 20 g Protein; 98 mg Sodium

lime chipotle flank steak with chipotle salsa

You'll want to use this wonderful, spicy salsa with everything from tortilla chips to hamburgers, but it really goes well with this tender, lime-infused steak.

CHIPOTLE SALSA

Olive oil	2 tbsp.	30 mL
Chopped sweet onion	1 1/2 cups	375 mL
Garlic cloves, minced	3	3
Fresh cilantro or parsley, lightly packed	1/3 cup	75 mL
Chopped chipotle peppers in adobo sauce (see Tip, page 64)	1 tsp.	5 mL
Large Roma (plum) tomatoes, quartered and seeds removed	6	6
Red wine vinegar	2 tbsp.	30 mL
Granulated sugar	1 tsp.	5 mL
Salt	1 tsp.	5 mL

LIME MARINADE

Lime juice (see Tip, page 64)	1/2 cup	125 mL
Grated lime zest	1 tbsp.	15 mL
Finely chopped chipotle peppers in adobo sauce (see Tip, page 64)	2 tsp.	10 mL
Garlic cloves, minced	3	3
Ground coriander	1 tsp.	5 mL
Ground cumin	1 tsp.	5 mL
Salt	1 tsp.	5 mL
Flank steak	1 1/2 lbs.	680 g

Chipotle Salsa: Heat olive oil in medium frying pan on medium. Add onion. Cook for 15 to 20 minutes, stirring often, until caramelized. Add garlic. Heat and stir for 1 to 2 minutes until fragrant.

Put cilantro and chipotle pepper into food processor. Process with on/off motion until coarsely chopped. Add tomato and onion mixture. Process with on/off motion until coarsely chopped. Transfer to medium bowl. Stir in next 3 ingredients. Let stand for 30 minutes to blend flavours. Makes about 2 cups (500 mL) salsa.

Lime Marinade: Combine all 7 ingredients in small bowl. Makes about 2/3 cup (150 mL) marinade.

Put steak into large resealable freezer bag. Add marinade. Seal bag. Turn until coated. Let stand in refrigerator for 2 to 3 hours, turning occasionally. Remove steak. Transfer marinade to small saucepan. Bring to a boil. Reduce heat to medium-low. Simmer, uncovered, for 5 minutes. Preheat gas barbecue to high. Cook steak on greased grill, turning once and brushing with reserved marinade, for about 5 minutes per side or until desired doneness. Transfer to cutting board. Cover with foil. Let stand for 10 minutes. Cut against the grain into very thin slices. Serve with Chipotle Salsa. Serves 6.

1 serving: 267 Calories; 13.1 g Total Fat (6.7 g Mono, 0.8 g Poly, 4.2 g Sat); 44 mg Cholesterol; 11 g Carbohydrate; 2 g Fibre; 27 g Protein; 855 mg Sodium

peppery balsamic steaks

*Marinades always contain an acid, such as the balsamic vinegar in this recipe.
Never use an aluminum dish to marinate meat, as the metal reacts with the
acid and can affect the taste.*

CHILI BALSAMIC MARINADE
Balsamic vinegar	3 tbsp.	50 mL
Liquid honey	3 tbsp.	50 mL
Dried crushed chilies	1/2 tsp.	2 mL
Beef top sirloin steak, cut into 4 pieces	1 lb.	454 g
Montreal steak spice	1 tsp.	5 mL

Chili Balsamic Marinade: Combine first 3 ingredients in small cup. Makes about
1/3 cup (125 mL) marinade.

Make shallow diagonal cuts about 1/2 inch (12 mm) apart on top of but not
through steak portions. Place steak in shallow baking dish. Pour marinade over
steak. Turn to coat. Let stand for 5 minutes. Arrange steak on greased broiler pan.
Transfer marinade to small saucepan. Bring to a boil. Reduce heat to medium-low.
Simmer, uncovered, for 5 minutes. Brush steaks with marinade.

Sprinkle with 1/2 tsp. (2 mL) steak spice. Broil on top rack in oven for 5 minutes.
Turn. Brush with boiled marinade. Sprinkle with remaining steak spice. Broil for
another 2 to 4 minutes until desired doneness. Serves 4.

*1 serving: 236 Calories; 8.1 g Total Fat (3.3 g Mono, 0.3 g Poly, 3.1 g Sat); 60 mg Cholesterol;
15 g Carbohydrate; trace Fibre; 24 g Protein; 174 mg Sodium*

zesty broiled steak

Toasting the sesame seeds brings out the oils and complements the orange in the marinade. This entree is ready to serve in about 30 minutes.

ORANGE ROSEMARY RUB

Soy sauce	1 tbsp.	15 mL
Garlic clove, minced (or 1/4 tsp., 1 mL, powder)	1	1
Grated orange zest	1 tsp.	5 mL
Dried rosemary, crushed	1/2 tsp.	2 mL
Beef top sirloin (or rib-eye or strip loin) steak	1/2 lb.	225 g

Sesame seeds, toasted (see Tip, page 64)

Orange Rosemary Rub: Combine first 4 ingredients in small cup. Makes about 1 1/2 tbsp. (25 mL) rub.

Spread rub on both sides of steak. Let stand for 10 minutes. Preheat broiler. Place steak on greased broiler pan. Broil on top rack in oven for 4 to 6 minutes per side until desired doneness. Transfer to cutting board. Cover with foil. Let stand for 10 minutes.

Sprinkle with sesame seeds. Serves 2.

1 serving: 142 Calories; 4.1 g Total Fat (2 g Mono, 0.5 g Poly, 1.7 g Sat); 53 mg Cholesterol; 2 g Carbohydrate; trace Fibre; 23 g Protein; 571 mg Sodium

grilled steak and vegetables

If you're broiling this sirloin use the centre rack and reduce the time to five to six minutes a side.

Fresh whole white mushrooms	18	18
Medium zucchini (with peel), cut into 1/2 inch (12 mm) thick slices	2	2
Medium red onion, cut into wedges	1	1
Medium red pepper, cut into wedges	1	1
Medium yellow pepper, cut into wedges	1	1
Light Italian dressing	3/4 cup	175 mL
CARAMEL CORIANDER RUB		
Brown sugar, packed	2 tbsp.	30 mL
Olive (or cooking) oil	1 tbsp.	15 mL
Garlic cloves, minced (or 3/4 tsp., 4 mL, powder)	3	3
Dry mustard	1 tsp.	5 mL
Ground coriander	1 tsp.	5 mL
Salt	1 tsp.	5 mL
Pepper	2 tsp.	10 mL
Beef top sirloin (flank or inside round) steak	2 lbs.	900 g

Put first 5 ingredients into large, resealable freezer bag. Add dressing. Seal bag. Turn to coat. Let stand in refrigerator for 2 to 3 hours, turning occasionally. Drain and discard marinade. Spread vegetable mixture evenly in large greased foil pan. Preheat gas barbecue to medium. Place pan on ungreased grill. Cook vegetables for 8 to 10 minutes, stirring occasionally, until tender-crisp. Remove from heat. Cover to keep warm.

Caramel Coriander Rub: Combine first 7 ingredients in small bowl. Makes about 1/3 cup (75 mL) rub.

Spread rub over both sides of steak. Reduce heat to medium-low. Cook steak on greased grill for 7 to 10 minutes per side until desired doneness. Transfer to cutting board. Cover with foil. Let stand for 10 minutes. Cut across the grain into 1/4 inch (6 mm) thick slices. Serve with vegetables. Serves 8.

1 serving: 217 Calories; 9.9 g Total Fat (4.7 g Mono, 0.7 g Poly, 3.2 g Sat); 50 mg Cholesterol; 12 g Carbohydrate; 2 g Fibre; 21 g Protein; 505 mg Sodium

chili-rubbed flank steak

Double or quadruple the spice rub ingredients so you can give some to the guests who will rave about this flavourful steak. The pinch of cinnamon gives it a Moroccan flavour.

CASBAH CHILI RUB		
Chili powder	1 tsp.	5 mL
Ground cumin	1/4 tsp.	1 mL
Salt	1/2 tsp.	2 mL
Pepper	1/4 tsp.	1 mL
Ground cinnamon, just a pinch		
Beef flank steak, trimmed of fat	1 lb.	454 g
Cooking spray		

Casbah Chili Rub: Combine first 5 ingredients in small cup. Makes about 2 tsp. (10 mL) rub.

Rub spice mixture into both sides of steak. Spray with cooking spray. Preheat gas barbecue to medium. Cook on greased grill for 4 to 6 minutes per side until desired doneness. Transfer to cutting board. Cover with foil. Let stand for 10 minutes. Cut steak across the grain into 1/4 inch (6 mm) thick slices. Serves 4.

1 serving: 191 Calories; 8.8 g Total Fat (3.6 g Mono, 0.4 g Poly, 3.7 g Sat); 46 mg Cholesterol; trace Carbohydrate; trace Fibre; 26 g Protein; 354 mg Sodium

mustard seasoned steak

We've paired this wonderful marinade with beef, but it also works well with lamb.

MUSTARD WINE MARINADE

Dijon mustard (with whole seeds)	1/4 cup	60 mL
Dry (or alcohol-free) white wine	1/4 cup	60 mL
Apple cider vinegar	2 tbsp.	30 mL
Cooking oil	2 tbsp.	30 mL
Finely chopped fresh rosemary	1 tbsp.	15 mL
(or 3/4 tsp., 4 mL, dried, crushed)		
Pepper, sprinkle		
Flank steak	1 1/2 lbs.	680 g

Mustard Wine Marinade: Combine first 6 ingredients in small bowl. Makes about 2/3 cup (150 mL) marinade.

Put steak into large resealable freezer bag. Add marinade. Seal bag. Turn to coat. Let stand in refrigerator for at least 6 hours or overnight, turning occasionally. Transfer marinade to small saucepan. Bring to a boil. Reduce heat to medium-low. Simmer, uncovered, for 5 minutes. Set aside. Preheat gas barbecue to high. Cook steak on greased grill for 5 to 7 minutes per side, turning occasionally and brushing with boiled marinade, until desired doneness. Transfer to cutting board. Cover with foil. Let stand for 10 minutes. Cut across the grain into very thin slices. Serves 6.

1 serving: 249 Calories; 14.1 g Total Fat (6.4 g Mono, 2.1 g Poly, 4.2 g Sat); 46 mg Cholesterol; 1 g Carbohydrate; 0 g Fibre; 27 g Protein; 198 mg Sodium

acapulco beef fillet

Make this in one frying pan, or save time by having two frying pans going at once: one for the veggies and the other for the steak.

Hard margarine (or butter)	1 tbsp.	15 mL
Large onion, thinly sliced	1	1
Medium red pepper, cut into 1 1/2 inch (3.8 cm) pieces	1	1
Medium yellow pepper, cut into 1 1/2 inch (3.8 cm) pieces	1	1
Prepared beef broth	1/2 cup	125 mL
Chili sauce	3 tbsp.	50 mL
Salt	1/2 tsp.	2 mL
Coarsely ground pepper	1 tsp.	5 mL
Coarsely ground pepper	2 tsp.	10 mL
Beef tenderloin steaks (about 4 oz., 113 g, each)	4	4
Cooking oil	1 tbsp.	15 mL
Tequila	2 tbsp.	30 mL
Lime juice	1 tbsp.	15 mL
Salt	1/4 tsp.	1 mL

Melt margarine in large frying pan on medium. Add onion. Cook for about 10 minutes, stirring often, until soft. Add red and yellow peppers. Cook for 2 to 3 minutes, stirring occasionally, until tender-crisp.

Add next 4 ingredients. Simmer, covered, for 7 minutes. Drain. Discard liquid. Transfer vegetables to serving platter. Cover to keep warm.

Rub second amount of pepper into both sides of steak. Heat cooking oil in same frying pan on medium-high. Add steaks. Cook for 3 to 4 minutes per side until desired doneness. Place steaks on top of warm vegetable mixture.

Combine tequila and lime juice in same frying pan. Simmer, uncovered, for 2 minutes. Add second amount of salt. Stir. Pour over steaks. Serves 4.

1 serving: 271 Calories; 13.7 g Total Fat (6.6 g Mono, 1.7 g Poly, 3.5 g Sat); 55 mg Cholesterol; 7 g Carbohydrate; 1 g Fibre; 25 g Protein; 768 mg Sodium

tenderloin with mixed peppercorn sauce

Tenderloin tastes best if rare or medium rare, so don't overcook it. To crack peppercorns easily, place them in an unsealed freezer bag and gently pound and roll the peppercorns with a rolling pin until cracked. Toss a few peppercorns on top as garnish just before serving.

Beef tenderloin steaks (about 4 oz., 113 g, each)	4	4
Whole mixed peppercorns, crushed	1 tsp.	5 mL
Cooking oil	2 tsp.	10 mL
Prepared beef broth	1/4 cup	60 mL
Gin	1 tbsp.	15 mL
Half-and-half cream	2 tbsp.	30 mL

Rub steaks with pepper. Heat cooking oil in large frying pan on medium-high. Cook steaks for 3 to 4 minutes per side until desired doneness. Transfer steaks to plate. Cover to keep warm.

Add broth and gin to same frying pan. Reduce heat to medium. Simmer, uncovered, for about 2 minutes, stirring occasionally, until reduced by half.

Add cream. Simmer for 2 minutes. Serve with steaks. Serves 4.

1 serving: 172 Calories; 9.7 g Total Fat (4.1 g Mono, 1.0 g Poly, 3.2 g Sat); 45 mg Cholesterol; 1 g Carbohydrate; trace Fibre; 18 g Protein; 131 mg Sodium

buttered steak and shrimp

Such a divinely decadent meal—steak drizzled with flavoured butter and topped with shrimp. All you need is a few grilled vegetables to complete this special meal.

HONEY MUSTARD BUTTER

Cooking oil	2 tsp.	10 mL
Finely chopped red onion	2 tbsp.	30 mL
Garlic clove, minced (or 1/4 tsp., 1 mL, powder)	1	1
Hard butter (or margarine), softened	1/3 cup	75 mL
Honey prepared mustard	2 tbsp.	30 mL
Chopped fresh parsley (or 3/4 tsp., 4 mL, flakes)	1 tbsp.	15 mL
Pepper	1/4 tsp.	1 mL

STEAK AND SHRIMP

Beef filet mignon (about 4 oz., 113 g, each)	4	4
Cooking oil	1 tbsp.	15 mL
Salt	1/4 tsp.	1 mL
Pepper	1/4 tsp.	1 mL
Uncooked large shrimp (peeled and deveined), tails intact	12	12

Honey Mustard Butter: Heat cooking oil in small saucepan on medium-low. Add onion and garlic. Cook for about 5 minutes, stirring often, until onion is softened. Transfer to small bowl. Cool.

Add remaining 4 ingredients. Stir well. Shape into 4 inch (10 cm) log. Wrap with waxed paper. Chill for 1 to 2 hours until firm. Cut into 1/2 inch (12 mm) rounds. Makes 8 rounds.

Steak and Shrimp: Brush both sides of each steak with cooking oil. Sprinkle with salt and pepper. Preheat gas barbecue to medium-high. Cook steaks on greased grill for about 7 minutes per side or until desired doneness. Transfer to plate. Cover with foil. Let stand for 10 minutes.

Cook shrimp on greased grill for about 2 minutes per side until pink and curled. Place 2 rounds of butter and 3 shrimp on top of each steak. Serves 4.

1 serving: 504 Calories; 36.8 g Total Fat (14.3 g Mono, 3.1 g Poly, 16.3 g Sat); 152 mg Cholesterol; 6 g Carbohydrate; trace Fibre; 37 g Protein; 464 mg Sodium

broiled herbed rouladen

Here's a fast way to get sizzle from a steak: roll it up and slide it under the broiler. Easily doubled, this recipe is ready in less than 15 minutes.

Dijon mustard	2 tbsp.	30 mL
Beef rouladen steaks (about 4 oz., 113 g, each) or top round steaks (1/4 inch, 6 mm, thick)	2	2
Finely chopped fresh parsley (or 1 1/2 tsp., 7 mL, flakes)	2 tbsp.	30 mL

Spread mustard on 1 side of each steak. Sprinkle with parsley. Roll up, jelly roll-style. Secure with wooden picks. Preheat broiler. Place rolls, seam-side down, in greased broiler pan. Broil on top rack in oven for 4 minutes. Turn. Broil for about 3 minutes until browned. Do not overcook. Cut rolls into 1/4 inch (6 mm) thick slices. Serves 2.

1 serving: 142 Calories; 3.9 g Total Fat (1.4 g Mono, 0.7 g Poly, 1.2 g Sat); 46 mg Cholesterol; 1 g Carbohydrate; trace Fibre; 25 g Protein; 261 mg Sodium

spicy sesame-crusted steak

We've paired this steak with a wonderful tropical salsa. Choose a papaya with a firm (never wrinkled) skin that gives slightly to palm pressure and is changing from green to yellow. Papayas will ripen at room temperature.

Sesame seeds	2 tbsp.	30 mL
Curry powder	1 tbsp.	15 mL
Coarsely ground pepper	2 tsp.	10 mL
Beef tenderloin steaks (about 4 oz., 113 g, each)	4	4
PAPAYA COCONUT SALSA		
Chopped papaya	1 cup	250 mL
Flaked coconut, toasted (see Tip, page 64)	1/4 cup	60 mL
Sweet (or regular) chili sauce	2 tbsp.	30 mL
Chopped fresh mint (or 3/4 tsp., 4 mL, dried)	1 tbsp.	15 mL
White wine vinegar	1 tbsp.	15 mL

Combine first 3 ingredients in shallow baking dish.

Preheat electric grill for 5 minutes. Press edges of steaks in sesame seed mixture until coated. Cook steaks on greased grill for 5 to 7 minutes per side until desired doneness. Transfer to plate. Cover with foil. Let stand for 10 minutes.

Papaya Coconut Salsa: Combine all 5 ingredients in small bowl. Makes about 1 1/4 cups (300 mL) salsa. Serve with steaks. Serves 4.

1 serving: 267 Calories; 13.8 g Total Fat (4.1 g Mono, 1.3 g Poly, 6.3 g Sat); 70 mg Cholesterol; 10 g Carbohydrate; 3 g Fibre; 25 g Protein; 302 mg Sodium

gourmet stuffed steak

If you marinate the steak the night before, this is a snap to make.

HERB MARINADE

Red wine vinegar	1/2 cup	125 mL
Infused herb (or cooking) oil	2 tbsp.	30 mL
Garlic clove, minced (or 1/4 tsp., 1 mL, powder)	1	1
Flank steak	1 1/2 lbs.	680 g

STUFFING

Frozen, chopped spinach, thawed and squeezed dry	5 oz.	140 g
Medium carrots, blanched and cut in half lengthwise	2	2
Small onions, blanched and sliced	2	2
Large hard-cooked eggs, quartered	2	2
Medium red pepper, sliced	1	1
Chopped fresh parsley (or 1 1/2 tsp., 7 mL, flakes)	2 tbsp.	30 mL
Salt	1/4 tsp.	1 mL
Pepper	1/8 tsp.	0.5 mL

GRAVY

Boiling water	4 cups	1 L
Beef bouillon powder	2 tbsp.	30 mL
Cold water	1 cup	250 mL
All-purpose flour	1/4 cup	60 mL
Salt	1/4 tsp.	1 mL
Pepper	1/8 tsp.	0.5 mL

Herb Marinade: Combine first
3 ingredients in small bowl. Makes about
2/3 cup (150 mL) marinade.

To butterfly steak, cut horizontally almost,
but not quite through, to other side. Open
flat. Place between 2 sheets of plastic
wrap. Pound with mallet or rolling pin to
1/4 inch (6 mm) thickness. Put steak into
resealable freezer bag. Add marinade. Seal
bag. Turn to coat. Let stand in refrigerator
for at least 6 hours or overnight, turning
once. Remove steak.

Stuffing: Layer all 8 ingredients, in order
given, over steak, leaving about 3 inch
(7.5 cm) edge from one long side. Roll up,
jelly-roll style, from opposite long side to
enclose stuffing. Tie with butcher's string
or secure with metal skewers. Place steak
on ungreased broiler pan. Broil on top rack
in oven for about 4 minutes per side, until
evenly browned. Place in medium roasting
pan. Do not place on rack.

Gravy: Combine boiling water and bouillon
powder in large bowl. Pour over steak.
Bake, covered, in 350°F (175°C) oven
for 1 1/2 hours, turning once so that top
does not dry out. Transfer to cutting board.
Cover with foil. Let stand for 10 minutes.
Measure 3 cups (750 mL) liquid from
roasting pan. Discard remaining liquid.
Skim and discard fat from reserved liquid.
Pour into small saucepan on medium.

Stir cold water into flour in small cup
until smooth. Add to liquid. Heat and stir
until boiling and thickened. Add salt and
pepper. Stir. Makes about 4 cups (1 L)
gravy. Cut steak across the grain into
1/2 inch (12 mm) thick slices. Serve with
stuffing and gravy. Serves 6.

1 serving: 280 Calories; 11.9 g Total Fat (4.9 g Mono, 1.0 g Poly, 4.4 g Sat); 118 mg Cholesterol; 13 g Carbohydrate; 2 g Fibre; 30 g Protein; 1210 mg Sodium

blue-cheese buttered steak

The blue-cheese butter can be stored in the freezer for up to a week; what an easy way to impress dinner guests!

BLUE-CHEESE BUTTER

Blue cheese, crumbled	2 tbsp.	30 mL
Butter (not margarine), softened	2 tbsp.	30 mL
Small garlic clove, minced (or 1/8 tsp., 0.5 mL, powder)	1	1
Dijon mustard	1/2 tsp.	2 mL
Worcestershire sauce	1/4 tsp.	1 mL
Beef rib-eye steak, cut into 4 pieces	1 lb.	454 g
Pepper, sprinkle		

Blue-Cheese Butter: Combine first 5 ingredients in small bowl. Spoon onto sheet of waxed paper. Shape into 2 inch (5 cm) long log. Wrap with waxed paper. Place in freezer until ready to serve. Makes about 1/2 cup (60 mL) butter.

Sprinkle both sides of steaks with pepper. Preheat electric grill for 5 minutes or gas barbecue to medium-high. Cook on greased grill for 5 to 6 minutes per side until desired doneness. Transfer to cutting board. Cover with foil. Let stand for 10 minutes. Unwrap blue cheese log. Cut into 4 equal pieces. Place steak portions on individual plates. Top with Blue-Cheese Butter slice. Serves 4.

1 serving: 333 Calories; 25.6 g Total Fat (10.1 g Mono, 0.9 g Poly, 11.9 g Sat); 79 mg Cholesterol; 1 g Carbohydrate; 0 g Fibre; 24 g Protein; 183 mg Sodium

holiday steak

Perfect for a long-weekend barbecue, or some cold winter evening when you want a culinary escape to a balmy climate.

PINEAPPLE SALSA

Can of pineapple tidbits, drained	19 oz.	540 mL
Chopped red onion	1 cup	250 mL
Chopped fresh cilantro or parsley	1/4 cup	60 mL
Lime juice	2 tbsp.	30 mL
Cayenne pepper	1/2 tsp.	2 mL

PINEAPPLE MARINADE

Steak sauce	2/3 cup	150 mL
Pineapple juice	1/2 cup	125 mL
Lime juice (see Tip, page 64)	1/4 cup	60 mL
Grated lime zest	1 tbsp.	15 mL
Dried oregano	1/2 tsp.	2 mL
Ground cumin	1/2 tsp.	2 mL
Cayenne pepper	1/4 tsp.	1 mL

STEAK

Beef top sirloin (or strip loin or rib) steak	2 lbs.	900 g
Garlic clove, cut in half	1	1

Pineapple Salsa: Combine all 5 ingredients in small bowl. Chill, covered, for at least 1 hour to blend flavours. Makes about 2 1/4 cups (550 mL) salsa.

Pineapple Marinade: Combine all 7 ingredients in small bowl. Stir well. Makes about 1 1/3 cups (375 mL) marinade.

Steak: Rub both sides of steak with cut sides of garlic clove. Put steak into large resealable freezer bag. Add marinade. Seal bag. Turn until coated. Let stand in refrigerator for 30 minutes, turning once. Remove steak. Transfer marinade to small saucepan. Bring to a boil. Reduce heat to medium-low. Simmer, uncovered for 5 minutes. Reserve half in small bowl. Preheat gas barbecue to medium-high. Cook steak on greased grill for 5 to 7 minutes per side, brushing often with remaining marinade, until desired doneness. Transfer to cutting board. Cover with foil. Let stand for 10 minutes. Spoon reserved marinade over steaks. Serve with salsa. Serves 6.

1 serving: 355 Calories; 16 g Total Fat (6.5 g Mono, 0.7 g Poly, 6.2 g Sat); 82 mg Cholesterol; 22 g Carbohydrate; 2 g Fibre; 30 g Protein; 452 mg Sodium

beef oscar

This succulent steak is topped with asparagus, crabmeat and a fast Hollandaise Sauce. Please see our raw egg tip at the back.

Water		
Fresh asparagus spears, trimmed of tough ends	16	16
Can of crabmeat, drained, cartilage removed and flaked	4 1/4 oz.	120 g
All-purpose flour	1/4 cup	60 mL
Salt	1/2 tsp.	2 mL
Pepper	1/8 tsp.	0.5 mL
Beef tenderloin steaks (about 4 oz., 113 g, each)	4	4
Cooking oil	2 tsp.	10 mL
Hard margarine (or butter)	2 tsp.	10 mL
JIFFY HOLLANDAISE SAUCE		
Egg yolks, large (see Tip, page 64)	3	3
Lemon juice	2 tbsp.	30 mL
Salt	1/4 tsp.	1 mL
Drops of hot pepper sauce	1	1
Butter (not margarine)	3/4 cup	175 mL

Pour water into large frying pan until about 1 inch (2.5 cm) deep. Bring to a boil. Add asparagus. Reduce heat to medium. Cook, covered, for about 4 minutes until tender-crisp. Drain. Cover to keep hot.

Heat crab for 5 to 10 minutes on medium-low in small saucepan. Cover to keep hot.

Combine next 3 ingredients on plate.

Press both sides of steaks into flour mixture until coated. Heat cooking oil and margarine in large frying pan on medium. Add steaks. Cook for 3 to 4 minutes per side until desired doneness. Transfer to 4 plates. Place 4 asparagus spears on each steak. Spoon crab over asparagus. Cover to keep warm.

Jiffy Hollandaise Sauce: Process first 4 ingredients in blender until smooth. Heat butter in small saucepan until bubbling. With motor running, very slowly pour butter in thin stream through hole in blender lid. Process until fluffy and thickened. Makes about 1 cup (250 mL) sauce. Spoon sauce over crab. Serves 4.

1 serving: 651 Calories; 53.2 g Total Fat (17.8 g Mono, 3.3 g Poly, 27.6 g Sat); 341 mg Cholesterol; 10 g Carbohydrate; 1 g Fibre; 34 g Protein; 1000 mg Sodium

salsa-stuffed steak

Like lots of spice in your life? Choose a hotter salsa for this quickly prepared entree. If you're planning to broil this steak, place the foil-lined pan on the centre rack. As always, use tongs, not a fork, to turn the steak.

Beef top sirloin (or strip loin or rib-eye) steak, cut into 4 pieces	1 1/2 lbs.	680 g
Small onion, finely chopped	1	1
Salsa	1/2 cup	125 mL
Garlic cloves, minced (or 1/2 tsp., 2 mL, powder)	2	2
Ground cumin (or dried oregano)	1 tsp.	5 mL
Pepper	1 tsp.	5 mL

Cut deep pocket into 1 side of each steak, almost but not quite through to other side.

Combine next 3 ingredients in small bowl. Spoon salsa mixture into pockets. Secure with metal skewers.

Sprinkle with cumin and pepper. Preheat gas barbecue to medium-low. Cook steak on greased grill for 5 to 7 minutes per side until desired doneness. Transfer to plate. Cover with foil. Let stand for 10 minutes. Serves 4.

1 serving: 224 Calories; 6.4 g Total Fat (2.7 g Mono, 0.3 g Poly, 2.4 g Sat); 80 mg Cholesterol; 6 g Carbohydrate; 1 g Fibre; 35 g Protein; 118 mg Sodium

recipe index

topical tips

Blanching fruit or veggies: Drop them in boiling water and cook until slightly soft, then submerge in ice water to stop the cooking process.

Eggs in the raw: This recipe uses raw eggs. Make sure to use fresh, clean Grade A eggs. Keep chilled and consume the same day it's prepared. Always discard leftovers. Pregnant women, young children or the elderly shouldn't eat anything containing raw egg.

Handling chipotle peppers: Chipotle chili peppers are smoked jalapeño peppers. Be sure to wash your hands after handling. To store any leftover chipotle chili peppers, divide into recipe-friendly portions and freeze, with sauce, in airtight containers for up to one year.

Toasting nuts, seeds or coconut: Cooking times will vary for each type of nut, so never toast them together. For small amounts, place ingredient in an ungreased shallow frying pan. Heat on medium for three to five minutes, stirring often, until golden. For larger amounts, spread ingredient evenly in an ungreased shallow pan. Bake in a 350°F (175°C) oven for five to 10 minutes, stirring or shaking often, until golden.

Zest first; juice second: When a recipe calls for grated zest and juice, it's easier to grate the lemon or lime first, then juice it. Be careful not to grate down to the pith (white part of the peel), which is bitter and best avoided.

Nutrition Information Guidelines

Each recipe is analyzed using the Canadian Nutrient File from Health Canada, which is based on the United States Department of Agriculture (USDA) Nutrient Database.

- If more than one ingredient is listed (such as "butter or hard margarine"), or if a range is given (1 – 2 tsp., 5 – 10 mL), only the first ingredient or first amount is analyzed.

- For meat, poultry and fish, the serving size per person is based on the recommended 4 oz. (113 g) uncooked weight (without bone), which is 2 – 3 oz. (57 – 85 g) cooked weight (without bone) — approximately the size of a deck of playing cards.

- Milk used is 1% M.F. (milk fat), unless otherwise stated.

- Cooking oil used is canola oil, unless otherwise stated.

- Ingredients indicating "sprinkle," "optional," or "for garnish" are not included in the nutrition information.

- The fat in recipes and combination foods can vary greatly depending on the sources and types of fats used in each specific ingredient. For these reasons, the count of saturated, monounsaturated and polyunsaturated fats may not add up to the total fat content.